My Beloved Child

My journey since the death of my daughter

ARLEAH SHECHTMAN

—

Fifth Wave Leadership Publications

ISBN: 1475046995
ISBN 13: 9781475046991

This book is dedicated to "my little sunshine"
Sharon Eileen
July 11, 1962 – April 13, 1978

When I was a child I had a favorite doll I named Sharon,
and I promised myself that if I ever had a little girl, I would
name her Sharon. I still have the doll.

Table of Contents

Preface

There are few, if any, experiences in life more devastating than the death of one's child. The agony of the loss, coupled with its protracted and seemingly endless grieving process, is what Arleah passionately shares in this remarkable book. She opens the very depths of her soul and her heart for all to see. Not as a martyr, but rather as a sensitive, loving, and very real woman gripped by the unexplained and undeserved, wondering what all this means for her and others with like experience.

She confronts the reader with her experience of primal loss, sharing, and yet teaching, too. Her discoveries need airing; all who suffer this level of loss need respite, but before that, they need something even more profound. They need to embrace the grief that pours out of a seemingly endless and primeval source. It is here that the learning and discoveries lie. In so doing, Arleah opens the doors to a hurt that often consumes more than one life, often for a lifetime. The energy, sorrow, anger, and hope implicitly and explicitly described are of an unfathomable magnitude.

This book is a story of real life; a story of a mother and her dearly loved child. It is a story of loss, but more importantly, a passionate and honest description of the process of internalizing and embracing the unimaginable nature of that loss. Arleah's journey will enlighten, comfort, and reveal that which all suffering parents encounter, but may not be able to put a name to.

Whatever your faith, your beliefs, or your values, Arleah speaks to you directly, lovingly, and with honesty unexpurgated. Experiencing this kind of loss reaches to all parents who have lost a child, but also to parents whose children are disabled, developmentally and/or physically, and for all those who try to engage with people experiencing these unimaginable hurts in their lives. This book is life affirming and is in itself an extraordinary statement of courage and love.

It IS a must-read; it is a tough read, and an emotional read, and, too, a deeply moving read. Yet this book opens us up to grieving as a process unto itself, a debate now raging in circles that wrestle with terminology and categorization. And, while grieving may be seen as belonging to those sick, Arleah's passionate description of her march to acceptance is moving, terrifying, and, in the end, perfectly understandable.

I have been blessed to know and care for Arleah and her equally remarkable husband for over thirty years. The two of them connected shortly after the disturbing events of the death of Arleah's daughter. As is true of many who face this level of trauma, it took in its wake Arleah's first marriage. Yet, as we believe, all things in life have purpose, so she found Morrie and/or he found her; a relationship I have witnessed, marveled at, and often been simply astounded by. It is Morrie that Arleah credits for being able to get through the agony of her loss; and it is Arleah that Morrie credits for a life-producing relationship that has kept them together; growing, loving, and re-creating the truly intimate marital relationship.

In their lives and their work, Arleah and Morrie have invested their curiosity, their gifts, and their energy in discovering ways to better live in a tumultuous world; a world rife with wonder and opportunity. And it is in this world, where a frightening pace of change is accompanied by near-constant and overwhelming loss, that the Shechtmans continue to thrive. It is their pioneering work on relationships (individual and corporate), and marriage, seen in their writing and consulting, that have profoundly impacted the lives of countless numbers of people like me and my dear wife, Judy Butterworth-Kremer.

The Shechtmans' challenge and confront us, because, you see, that is what love and commitment are all about. We have learned that; I have, with certainty. We encourage all readers to take a swim; it may feel a bit like being thrown into the pool as a young-ster, but it is likely that the dousing will open new possibilities in your own lives.

Respectfully,

Reverend Richard H. Kremer
Gloria Dei Lutheran Church
Providence, RI

Acknowledgments

My journey back from a puddle by her grave has been possible because Morrie wouldn't allow me to die with her. He prevented that desire in me by caring enough to keep challenging me. That I chose to let that happen is why this story is thirty-plus years old. I am forever grateful for our partnership. Throughout these years we have been through many other challenges, losses, and hard times. All this has been easier with Morrie on my side and by my side. He has never wavered from his faith in my value and in me. He is the only person that has hung in with my terrible struggle to recover, year after year, decade after decade. He has insisted over the years that my poems and story can be helpful to others. This is my attempt to fulfill his faith in me.

No one has been more supportive, loving, and demanding than Morrie Shechtman, and from this honing of our lives together we have developed a different way of working with people. The difference is captured in our other books.

My deepest gratitude also goes to Deb Newell, who came into my life much later. She is one of the few others with whom I have shared the poems and much of the story. Deb has never turned away from my pain, but has helped me relearn to celebrate and laugh.

I appreciate Carrie Thiel, who did some of the early editing and asked many questions that sent me back to rewrite whole sections.

She often stated that she wanted to know more about some aspect of my journey or another.

My brothers and their families have all been important parts of my life and journey. My children have been supportive also.

Then there are those that knew nothing of my journey or were not in my inner circle that helped without knowing, simply by caring for me.

Introduction

This is the story of my journey since the death of my daughter. I'm not really sure why writing about the death of my daughter and my journey of recovery has suddenly become so important after this many years. Her life and death are so much a part of the fabric of my being that it is hard to step back and write about it. I feel that most of my other work is almost done and this is not. In the long run, there is no logic as to why, because this is not about logic, it's just about my feelings.

I did a little research—thank you, Google—and discovered that roughly 1,600,000 children between the ages of zero and nineteen die each year. That is only about 0.5 percent of the population, but to each of those families it's the only thing that counts.

I figured that since the time of my personal tragedy, over fifty million families have experienced the loss of a child. I feel that is an underserved population, basically due to the strong injunctions against grieving, which include people's reluctance to burden others with their problems. I also think there is always room for one more voice that will reach someone. There were, and continue to be, so many voices, writings, movies, and open arms that helped me during this long journey. I can never repay all those gifts; all I can do is turn around and try to pass them on.

I put
My grief
On a shelf
In the
Back of
my heart
in Saran Wrap
bundles
so I can
feel safe
after thirty
years of
grief

Of course
I am not

Nothing is
Strong
Enough
To
Hold it
back
for very long

This is one of many poems I felt compelled to write, starting about eight months after Sharon's death. There was no thought or plan; they just came rushing out as fast as I could write them in this unusual form on a yellow notepad. That happened three different times during the first year, and has been an important avenue for expressing my grief. I have woven them throughout the book and include them in their entirety in a separate chapter at the end.

CHAPTER I

First Five Years: Chaos

and Reorienting

I am astonished
by how
stunned
broken
wounded
I am
by my child's death

I am astonished
by the
depth
breadth
pervasiveness
of my
pain in her loss

I am astonished
by how
the loss
of love
hurts

I am astonished
by how
living
love
heals

On April 13, 1978, I came home and found my fifteen-year-old daughter's body and I went mad. I knew the instant I touched her that there was no life in her body. Sharon had been dead for several hours so *livor mortis* had occurred. She was all blotchy and discolored. I ran around screaming, I don't know for how long; could have been a few minutes or a few hours. I could not think how to call the police. I still sometimes wake up screaming, as though it were just yesterday instead of over thirty years ago. It has been a long, tough journey back from that day. This is the narrative of that journey. Many have been there with me, and many have not. The death of a child is hard for everyone.

What came with this event was gross disorientation; shock to my very core and denial that this could be true. Denial was a good thing; the grief would have simply swamped me if it had come all at once. It still comes in huge, unmanageable waves, like throwing up with the flu. I have very little control at the crest of each wave. Grieving and vomiting serve the same purpose: to rid the body of pain. I hate doing either.

Grieving makes life different than before. An invisible force field is crossed, and there is no way back. One slips into grief silently, unnoticed by those left behind on the other side. I was not prepared for my own intense pain and shock. There is no way to prepare or plan for that road ahead; not that there ever was, but this is different. There is no way to fully share that experience; it is nearly wordless. The physical signs are somewhat apparent, though not all; like what felt like a hole in my middle, or the extreme waves of overwhelming crying, wailing.

The internal journey is harder to observe or articulate. Perhaps you can't truly know unless you've been there; a little like sharing the experience of an earthquake. You can talk about it, but can't share the experience of the very earth moving under your feet. So, who wants to talk about or hear about anything as unpleasant as the woe of my grievous loss? I don't know if anybody does; I only know that I need to say it. I suppose those who are on this side of the force field would like to know they aren't alone or weird; I did. For those that haven't arrived, I hope you never do.

I didn't experience "phases of grief;" I just felt overwhelming pain. The phases of grief are: shock and denial, bargaining, anger, depression, and acceptance. I wish I could be like those people who put their grief somewhere else and never shed a tear. I grieved loudly and often for at least the first year, upsetting many folks that wanted me to shut up and take some pills. That always seemed like a dishonoring of my daughter and her life. She was that dear to me. Not grieving her death would have been to discount that. The stress of being stoic is immense, and a killer of those who choose not to grieve.

That was choice number one on the long journey back from destroyed to rebuilt: simply to grieve.

Grieving is not something we have to learn; it comes with the package, and it is part of the human condition. Evidently, it is an evolutionary mechanism for humans to be able to deal with the pain of grievous loss. We learn to recognize the symptoms and stages. The really hard part is to learn how to express our grief in ways that are healing. Who wants to be sad in such a chirpy culture as ours? Better not to say anything and suffer in silence. But that brings its own problems.

The choice to grieve has changed my life and opened a world I could not have known in any other way. I was in graduate school at the time of Sharon's death and received my Masters of Social Work the next June. As strange as it sounds, my career as a therapist and then later as an executive coach has been shaped and enriched by my loss.

But I am getting way ahead of myself. The journey back is always about relationships, and the conflict and disappointments inherent in a million choices along the way. Because of the way Sharon died, a drug overdose, the shame and remorse I felt were sometimes debilitating. It was never clear whether she died on purpose or not. If she did it intentionally, that was one grief; if it was an accident, that meant an entirely different type of grief. Sharon had come to me a few months before and told me that she was struggling with PCP and alcohol. She and I were in counseling together at the time of her death, so perhaps that would have meant we were succeeding. The confusion made my guilt especially persistent and difficult. I felt constantly tortured that I had failed to do something to help her choose to live.

Your Precious life
is gone,
some

by your own
hand.

Why?
I do not understand.

I am humbled
by
my own
limitations
that
I
could not
help you want
to live.

I am defeated
by
my own
pain, &
still
I
do not accept
what you said
about me.

It has always been difficult to write or talk about Sharon, my child, because the memories are still so intense and sharp; time has not changed that. She was, of course, the most beautiful baby in the world, and the cutest little girl. Unfortunately, we were at odds from the beginning. We were both strong willed and obstinate. I had trouble opening my heart to her because I didn't trust females at that time in my life, including myself. Nevertheless, she was my "sunshine," and brightened the corners of my life with love and laughter. Picking a flower from the neighbors' garden got her scolded by them and a smile from me. I remember when I was selling Avon; she was about three and trailed far behind me. She would get angry and shout, "Mommy, you have to keep up with me!" So many memories of her…

She started rebelling in first grade. Sharon hated the rigidity of the school day and the arbitrariness of school itself. She could never understand why she couldn't do her work in her own time and in her own way. She would line up her dolls and stuffed animals and admonish them for their bad behavior: "Stop talking. Sit still. No giggling." And on and on it would go. I'm sure she was repeating what she went through in school every day. In so many ways she was just a kid, like millions of others. But she was my kid, and that makes everything different.

Sharon was obsessively fond of dill pickles. It got to be a family joke; everywhere we went to eat, the refrain always was, "Are you going to eat your pickles? Can I have them?" I remember kidding her that she might turn green and smell like dill someday if she kept this up. She didn't mind, just kept eating pickles. Her favorite part of every birthday was the Costco-size jar of pickles she always got. Sometimes that jar even lasted an entire day.

Sharon sucked her thumb from day one, another family secret. Whenever she was fussy or unhappy someone inevitably told her to "plug in," which usually worked. When Sharon turned six, she decided that she was going to learn to ride her bike with no training wheels and stop sucking her thumb before she started first grade. "I'm not going to be a big girl and still suck my thumb. That's for babies," she informed me, one hand on her hip and her lip stuck out defiantly. "I don't need training wheels anymore either, so just take them off, right now, so I can practice." I obligingly took them off, and she accomplished both goals before that September. Sharon was a very determined little girl. If she made up her mind to accomplish something she usually did. That's probably how she got from Illinois to Ohio on her own when she was twelve. The one thing we both failed at was to reconcile our differences.

I hear
your
laughter
see your
smile,
in
my memory
in
my mind

I
don't
want
a
memory.

I
want you
alive.

As she grew into a teenager, she began to drift in a wrong direction, toward drinking, drugs, and sex. She ran away at twelve (even before adolescence) and somehow ended up in Ohio, from

Illinois, at my brother Larry's with her cousins Charisa and Ric. They agreed to let her stay for a while. All the long night she was gone, with no word of her whereabouts, her father basically washed his hands of the whole deal and said it was up to me to handle it. Her place and mine in that family were one step below the basement. Her older brother, David, was lost in the middle somewhere. This was a very stratified, mostly chaotic, and unhappy family. The pain of her death finished the fracturing.

Expanded consciousness
is simply
dealing
with
the
pain
&
living
my
life.

I am able
to be
reduced
to raw, open
pain
&
come back
whole.

So many memories of her sweetness, her cute sayings, and the feel of holding her as she grew up. So many memories of our quarrels and shouting matches; the frustration, exasperation, and disappointment with myself that I can never rectify or make better. Sharon loved me fiercely, and I her. I just had trouble expressing my love in a coherent way that she could understand. I was lamenting my failures one day to a friend, that I should have been kinder, more patient, etc. My friend gently said, "You were raising her to live, not to die. All parents are imperfect." Another small choice to let go of trying to control that which I had lost.

Guilt was my constant companion throughout my recovery, accentuated by the question of cause. The critic always interrupted the internal narrative of "maybe this" or "maybe that" with "No, no, no! You were her mother, and you are responsible. It was your job. You are just making excuses for yourself!" An enormous part of the gut-wrenching guilt was the relationship we had. It was often adversarial and full of conflict. I have never been able to say all the things I've heard and read that other parents say after the death of their child. Neither she nor I were angels. We were often at war. I have spent a great deal of time over the years regretting that rift and longing for "another chance."

I remember one bad day a few months after her death, when I was going around in circles internally about my responsibility. I could find no way or answer that didn't lead back to me. I was asking myself if I had killed my child. I was lamenting that with Morrie (my husband, not her father) and he said, "What if you did? What should happen to you?" His questions were both a shock and a kindness.

I agonized, trying to find the answers to Morrie's questions. So, what should happen to me? Should I be tried for murder? Or executed for my complicity in her death? The agony was intense. I could find no way out. Then it slowly dawned on me that, as her mother, of course I had a large part in her life and death, but I am not omnipotent. There were many other people in her life; I was not an island. The startling realization I came to was that Sharon had other choices, choices that didn't rely only on me. It certainly was her choice to use drugs at all. That was another choice point for me, not to stay lost in the guilt.

Morrie's statement was indeed a shock and a gift. It took the shock to unstick me, and the kindness was his faith that I could work through the angst. He had great confidence in my resilience and my ability to handle even this earthquake. Out of that crucible of pain and guilt, I have learned to trust that resilience in others and myself. I am still grateful for Morrie's faith in me.

After all these years, some memories are as vivid as if they happened yesterday, and others are very fuzzy. The vivid memories are probably important choice points along the way. I remember Sharon's funeral and burial as nightmares. Picking her casket was a horror show. They were lined up like used cars and the salesperson boasted about the attributes of each. If I chose this coffin, her body would last longer because it had a better seal, while that one was less well sealed. There was the color of the inside to consider, the type of blanket, and, of course, the outside: wood or metal. I don't know how else it can be done, but that was horrendous. I'm glad I was still in shock and denial. I no longer know how I made that decision or why I chose a particular one over another. I vaguely remember pointing and saying, "That one is fine." Then collapsing into a puddle of grief. The choice here was to get up at all.

Other vivid memories are of the number of people who wanted me to be stoic and not upset them. Several offered me Valium, or to pray with me. I have nothing against either when not used to stop the grieving process. Each of those offers represented, in my mind, my chance to grieve or to cop out of my truth. I remember the day I buried my only daughter, the minister said, "OK, it's over, now buck up and get on with it." I was in no shape to respond or defend myself, so I just hurt harder and felt guiltier that I couldn't stop my grief. How to capture in words the moments at her funeral—of songs, of mouths moving with no meaning, of my mind and body in convulsions of protest, disbelief, and horror that this was it. No more fights, no more chances to make it better, just the end of life. Burying Sharon was the hardest thing I have ever had to do, and that day is still the most important of my memorial days. Burying my child buried a part of the purpose and meaning for my life. The hole in my soul took a long time to fill. This was not a dramatic event, or even visible. The filling was like the regrowth of life after a volcanic eruption. It was more like a tiny green fern sprouting on a desolate black landscape of hardened lava. The choice to find new meaning and purpose headed me in a direction of creativity and growth that I pursue to this day.

A newly bereaved person needs an advocate because she is just not "with it" for months. Another of those small choices that proved to be far reaching came after the funeral. Both Morrie and I were just tired. He made the absurd suggestion of, "Why don't we stop at Burger King and just be alone for a minute?" At that moment anything was fine with me, just stop the world. So that is what we did—had a burger, fries, and a Coke. Those few moments allowed me to regroup enough to go on. That incident was the beginning of a pattern that still works for me: the intense grieving followed by something mundane and "normal." If I ignore the feelings, then I never get the mundane and normal, because those intense feelings are always trying to escape.

I have learned over the years that my grief upsets most folks that haven't dealt with their own, and my sadness triggers theirs. The further one gets from the funeral, the less tolerance others have for one's grief. "Shouldn't you be over it by now?" is the most common question. What an absurd and insulting statement. Bereavement is a condition that never clears up. The loss of a child is a never-ending process of feeling wounded and regaining wholeness. Telling grieving parents to get over their grief would be like telling an amputee not to miss her arm.

Sometimes
I am
reduced to
nothing
but
my
grief at
loving &
missing
her.

When I am
able
to
let that
be,
I rise,
like
the
Phoenix.

Sometimes,
it is
very
hard

It has been my experience that grief comes in succeeding waves. When I could ride the wave to the crest and express whatever was there, the wave ebbed, and in between the waves I could live for a while. Surprisingly, the intense bouts were relatively short. I don't think they ever lasted even ten minutes. I learned this important lesson because I happened to be in primal therapy at the time of Sharon's death. The core thrust of this therapy is deep grief; it was permitted and encouraged. Even so, my expressions were very primitive, because the loss of a child is, well, primal. Primal feelings are wordless, with the intensity of a race car driver's focus, and almost that loud, like a Formula One car. The wailing and keening has a quality that goes below any thoughts or concepts, more like a wolf howling, that communicates everything without any words. It was a surprise to me that after the grief bout I usually found words and concepts to use with my clients as they struggled to express their feelings. That was a bonus I never expected. People—clients and friends—have often asked me what is to be gained by crying or screaming or any overt expression of distress. Part of the answer is that there develops a continuity and context for all the mysterious stuff we feel and do. Out of the feelings come the answers to the whys.

As I continued to trust my process, the waves gradually became farther apart, less intense, and not so devastating. I had spent a lifetime controlling my intense emotions, so my grief was very disturbing; I felt so out of control. And of course I was. Those terrible, out-of-control incidents were about the realignment of my reality and reorienting of my internal compass. In the face of death, we are so out of control and are completely inept; a very helpless, hopeless feeling. I remember feeling that all over again about fifteen years later, when visiting Morrie's dad as he was battling pancreatic cancer. Standing there by his bedside, I felt completely incompetent and inept unable to do one single thing to help him. Learning how to manage the enormity of all the upheaval connected to Sharon's death has profoundly changed me, and those that lived through it with me.

I have learned over the years that there is more out of my control than is within my control, and that my only true freedom is in how I choose to deal with the vicissitudes of life.

Again, the choice to stumble on has been an important component of my healing.

Another critical choice point came about two years after Sharon's death. I was in a conversation with a friend of mine, who interrupted whatever I was saying and said, "You know, Arleah, you use her death like a black ace. Trumps everyone else's problems and shuts everyone out." Well, that was another one of those hideous kicks in the gut. He was correct, of course. The choice here was whether to take the risk of loving again, or to attempt to stay safe. To reengage in life or keep my distance, knowing that I could lose again. That is one of the hardest choices any of us has to make after a major life-changing event.

Her death is
no
guarantee,
no insurance,
that I
will
not
lose again.

There is no
way
to
protect myself
from
further loss.

That is deeply
frightening.

What do
I
do with
that?

Well,
I guess
I
notice
how precious
today is
&
how deeply
I love you

Very few friends or family have the courage to confront a
grieving parent as my friend did, and as my husband had earlier.
It would have been easier for me to have told both of them to get
lost, to just leave me alone. It would have been less risky for them

to stay quiet. They couldn't understand my pain or what I was going through. That part is true, but I am glad they cared enough about me to engage in that conflict. I am glad I chose to come out of my hidey-hole and risk loving again. Whatever time is left for my loving, it is better than the bitter loneliness of isolation and the emotional, physical, and spiritual shutdown that the numbness of disengagement requires. I'll take anxiety any day over the dead zone.

Sometime during this early part of my journey, Morrie conveyed the message to me that while he loved me dearly and understood my pain, he just couldn't listen anymore, right then. Here was another difficult choice. I had to find people that could listen, right then. I developed a list of about ten folks I trusted and would call, one by one, to see if they were up to my grief, right then. There was always someone on my list who was there with comfort and solace. Grief requires comfort, a hard thing to keep asking for. Grief is one of those feelings that just goes on and on, far beyond what anyone wants. Everyone gets sick of it, including the one grieving, and still it continues. I never thought weariness was a good excuse for me to turn away or shut down. I just keep hanging in there because I know the grief will eventually recede like the waves on a beach.

CHAPTER 2

Ten Years: Realignment

and Acceptance

Many years after Sharon's death I had become so weary of grieving, so tired of the focus and drain on me, that I decided I was
done. I thought maybe everyone was right and I should be over it
by then. So I stopped all the remembrances I had created over the
years for the days that had been important in our lives together.
Around the anniversary of her death and burial, I didn't go to the
cemetery that year. I felt some pride and relief in that decision.
I felt pride and relief, that is, until I started hearing from family
and friends. Morrie especially kept asking, "What's wrong with
you? We have done nothing to deserve all the anger you are taking
out on us. So what's wrong?" I was surprised and hurt; I didn't
think anything was wrong. It took me a couple of days to make the
connection that my odd behavior was related to the choice not to
grieve. Nothing turns to hostility quicker than suppressed grief. I
have learned that I must honor those days in some way every year

or I get lost from myself, and usually take it out on someone else. The acknowledgement doesn't have to be big, or long, or dramatic; it just has to be honored.

During this time, I worked with an alternative high school for behavior disordered adolescents, or acting out kids. I went in guessing that somewhere between 40 percent and 60 percent of them would have had a significant loss closely associated with the acting out behavior. It turned out to be 99 percent. The other one percent I didn't have background information on. As I worked with these young people, teaching them new skills, many were able to start making different, more productive choices as they worked through their grief. I primarily helped them to recognize their own grief and the form that it took when they didn't honor it. Most of the work was done while playing pool (I got pretty good), as grief is a process and not an event. One important lesson in that experience was how hard it is for people, especially adolescents, to connect the dots between feelings and behavior, and how much harder it is to articulate them. A lot of the success of that program was my ability to hang out and hang in, mostly in indirect ways, like playing pool. I have developed almost infinite patience for grieving people. The comment I heard most pervasively throughout the two years I was there was, "You know, Ms. Shechtman, I'd rather get in a fistfight than deal with this stuff." Emotional pain is harder to deal with than physical pain, seemingly even more so for males in this culture. Throughout my career as a therapist and as an executive coach, the lament I hear from men is, "I'll do anything you ask, just don't make me cry." That makes me want to cry for them. No wonder there are so many angry men.

The loss of a child is very traumatic for the entire family, friends, and community. The statistics are alarming for marriages. Something like 90 percent of marriages are in trouble within months after that loss. Of the 90 percent, about half will make it through and at least stay together. There are few studies that I am aware of as to what happens within a relationship that has been so disrupted. But it has been my experience that the tragedy of the loss of a child destroys many myths about marriage and causes a profound existential crisis. The notion of "we are one" is very hard to maintain, as each partner must grieve in his or her own time and his or her own way. It is very unlikely that the individuals will be in sync in their grieving process. The very person we count on for solace and comfort is too upset to be available to us. This is disorienting in its own right, let alone combined with the grief of the death itself. There is often a lot of blaming back and forth, and feeling incensed that the other partner doesn't understand.

I remember feeling mostly annoyed at Sharon's father because he felt so "clingy." He was, of course, expecting the old, familiar reaction from me, and I from him. At that time our relationship was in serious trouble for other reasons. Any hope of reconciliation died with our daughter. I still have difficulty sorting out all those losses. Several years later, I asked my son David, Sharon's brother, if I had been helpful to him. His reply was, "Not even close." I really thought I was. The whole family system comes unglued, and must reconfigure without the absent dear one.

Over the years I have worked with and encountered many individuals that have lost a child, a sibling, or a grandchild. I am not surprised by how many families "die" when one of their children does. It seems to be especially hard on siblings because they often lose everything all at once. The sibling is gone, and the parents are so traumatized they can't help their other kids deal with the loss. Certainly, the family as everyone knew it is gone. A new family can, and often does, emerge, but the process is painful and requires a vehicle, like ceremonies, rites, or rituals, to allow everyone to grieve. Since no one grieves exactly like anyone else, various family members miss each other's signals, which increases the depth of the struggle.

One of the difficult choices embodied in the changes in my family was the choice to leave a marriage and go down a whole different path. It was the end of Sharon's father's and my hopes and dreams together. No one starts a marriage with the goal of divorce; we all start out a bit starry-eyed and determined to realize our dreams. He and I worked on that relationship for eighteen years, but the dream didn't hold up and we moved in different directions.

I spent hours at the cemetery, by Sharon's graveside. It is almost the only place where I could cry and not bother anyone else. Even there, often someone would ask me if I was all right. What a strange question. A cemetery is not a place I go when I am all right. As the weeks, months, and years passed, the nature and need of those visits changed. I learned a lot about myself during those long, lonely vigils.

When there

is

no one

there

for

me.

When I

must

face

her death

all alone.

When I
find
her dead
again & again.
That is when
I
know
who
I am.

I learned that my grief was about more than her death. I learned the difference between acute and chronic grief. When the feelings were just about her, the wailing was intense and surprisingly brief. Acute grief is the normal, natural process that people move through. The first year is the hardest, because it is the anniversary year. Each holiday or special time is the first without the lost person, lost job, lost community, or whatever the particular loss might be.

What makes grief so mysterious and hard is that it cuts right through all the defenses and touches our core. It touches all other grief and unresolved issues, and brings them to the surface along with the current grief. This is chronic grief. The feelings get stuck, and nothing ever feels better or resolved. That is what causes the sense of being out of control and feeling crazy. If there are significant unresolved issues, the defensive system goes into overdrive and a person gets stuck. Much like a record, just going round and round in the same phase.

I learned this quite by accident during a particularly difficult day, when I simply couldn't seem to get through the pain. I remember finally just sitting down in exhaustion and letting my mind wander. I found myself drifting to an old memory of myself as a child, alone and scared, with no one to comfort me. As I sat with that memory and let its sadness merge with me, the heaviness started to lift and I could go home. I needed to grieve for that old wound also. In working with people over the years, I have seen that intense loss cuts through all our carefully built walls and drags up other unhealed wounds. This is one of the reasons we avoid grief, and why it takes so long to recover. During this time period, I realized that no one could really go there with me, nor was there enough "help" to make it "all right." I share my life with many wonderful and important people, but there is that part of me that will always be alone, and grieve alone.

You cannot
know
what it's
like
to
have lost
a
beloved child.

You don't
have to
it is
enough
to
hold me
tight
&
let me
cry.

I remember feeling angry and upset that people just weren't being helpful enough. After the first year or year and a half, I realized that people had been there and there was enough help. It had just taken that long to work its magic. Healing was a process, not an event. That is the most common question my grieving clients ask: "When will I be better?" It's sort of like an open wound; it takes time to heal. Help is analogous to salve on that wound. Over time, the salve and the power of one's own body will heal the wound, but there will always be the scar.

> Your death has
> split me
> wide open,
> I am gutted
> like a steer
> freshly slaughtered.

> Your death
> has spared me
> nothing
> in horror,
> in terror.
> in guilt.

> What I didn't expect,
> had no way
> of knowing,
> was that the
> depth I
> plummeted to
> would

also find
new depths of
living
&
loving
&
laughter.

This has always been the tension; the terrible grief countered by the healing thrust. Ten years out was sort of nowhere land. The grief still dominated much of my thinking and feelings. I was beginning to back off from mentioning my bereavement with new acquaintances because it just didn't come up as often. Time does make a difference. I had found Compassionate Friends and other support groups helpful for quite a while, but at some point I just moved on. I remember so many other parents during that time. One mother I got to know pretty well captured the longing of most of us. Her eighteen-year-old son was killed trying to beat a train at the crossing. She so wanted to go back and do that day over. She had a thousand things that, if she had done or not done, would have changed the timing and he would still be alive. I, too, have wished that, over and over, just one small thing done or said differently would have changed things. That was the topic of conversations for years, the "if onlys" and the "what ifs," the terrible pain of wondering if it could have been different, but knowing it never would be. We often clung to each other like we were drowning, and I guess in a way we were. We were always searching for relief and redemption.

By this time I had remarried, to Morrie and had a third child, Charlie, and he took much of my attention and energy. The choice to take a chance on love and marriage, and a subsequent child, was full of guilt, anguish, and self-doubt. How could I be happy ever again? The trouble was that there was no one to really give me comfort and advice (except Morrie), since no one was interested in my struggles, nor my ongoing grief. The ability to love again, to raise my eyes and look around, to see joy and possibilities, was a conscious one, a deeply internal choice to live and not die with her. The result has been the happiest years of my life. Just because I have been in both places, the contrast is startling. Oddly, the decision to have another child was to celebrate that happiness is possible in the face of tragedy.

My blasphemy

is

that

I

can

no longer

remain

distraught.

Is that

a

betrayal

of

her?

We were all caught up in our lives. Sharon and her death were far away from this new life, if not from my heart. For a very long time, I had an ongoing image of myself with all these strings reaching out of my chest and belly, still connected to her. Sort of like an old-timey telephone operator with the phone lines—plugging, unplugging, and re-plugging the transmissions. It was my job to disconnect each of those wires connected to her and cauterize the ends. I could never find all the ends, though; some still dangle. There was a strong sense of something unfinished. So much does go unfinished when a life is cut short. I never got to launch her into adulthood, or be a part of her choices for her life.

I guess
I thought
the
depth of
my
grief
was
some measure
of
my love
for
her.

A tiny voice.
deep inside
whispers-
"Living
your life
is
the
only possible
answer
to
death."

An internal conflict has characterized much of my journey back, my recovery. I cannot forget and I cannot stay in the past. I found it sometimes very confusing to decide what to tell people about Sharon's death; to whom, and when. This was especially true with Charlie, the little boy we had. How much to tell him and when. I send a special salute to the child or children born after the death of a sibling, or who have survived that death. I wanted so much not to burden him with the heaviness of my sorrow. I failed at that because it is just a part of me. I never kept it a secret or turned away from his questions; it's just that I was not always as available as I tried to be.

The angst of Sharon's death is interwoven in every relationship and endeavor I undertake. I have accepted the fact that she is never coming back and I will never be the same. One very clear shift during those first ten years was an increasing intolerance for trivia and BS. I have been too raw and broken for niceties to have any meaning or solace. I know that has made it hard for some folks to be around me. Actually, that is fine with me, as I no longer know how to be "nice."

> Anguish
> Agony.
> Screaming pain.

> That is my world
> my universe.

> How do I survive?
> Why do I want to?

> Because
> You are there

I had an active practice of psychotherapy by this time, and found that my loss and recovery was a strange asset in my connecting with and helping others to heal. I could especially see the long-term effects of unexpressed grief. I could spot a fellow bereaved parent at a hundred yards. Something about the way they hold themselves, some vibe that connects with mine.

In addition to my practice, Morrie was building his business, which is helping CEOs deal with the interface between their personal and professional lives. One day he sat me down and asked, "How does grief get played out in business?" It took some time to apply all the stages and ramifications to that arena, but that is an integral part of what we do in our work together. It has proven to be both difficult and successful. Grieving is an ongoing process in the current economic world, as everyone has had to change rapidly and radically. And the requirement to keep changing, and therefore grieving, is only going to accelerate.

CHAPTER 3

Fifteen Years:

Weariness and Shutdown

Sometimes it was hard to keep things clear and straight after fifteen years of telling my story. I began to feel trite and lost. Fifteen was the anniversary where the years Sharon had been gone equaled the years of her life. I could no longer project what she might have been like by then. She was frozen in my memory at fifteen. The persistent feeling is hard to articulate, but was a protest that it had been so long since I had seen her. For the ten thousandth time, I chose to go on. No one wanted to hear about my grief anymore; in fact, very few even remembered the dates. I had moved away from her home, and hardly anyone in my current life had even known her.

Life feels
futile
&
sometimes absurd.

Why then
do I
go on?

Because, I
love
this world
&
have
to know
what
tomorrow holds.

I began to retreat from mentioning Sharon much at all. When new people would ask me how many children I had, I began to skip over her death, respond that we had three boys, and quickly change the subject. It felt terrible, but the alternative felt even worse at that time in my recovery. The choice here was to quietly withdraw and batten down the hatches. Sometimes grief is an exhausting journey. The problem was that many folks would respond that it was too bad I hadn't had the joy of a girl, so the truth usually came out anyway. It doesn't seem to matter if the story is told up front or later on; it so dominates the conversation that other issues and considerations often get sidelined.

I don't know exactly why this time was so difficult. It may have been that we left Illinois and moved to Montana, so I had to leave the only tie I had left to her—her grave. In retrospect, it seems like this was just another cycle in the never-ending "grieving process"; this particular time, the phase of bargaining. I just wanted to feel safe for a while and not engage, or be close to anyone. It is hard to articulate that long-term weariness. Like so many that are "different" and don't quite fit anywhere, I only wanted to be like everyone else. Being a bereaved parent is unusual, but being up front and vocal about it scares people, or puts them off. There is no all-purpose good choice in this arena, so it becomes a choice every time I meet someone new as to how to handle discussing that part of my life.

There was often some sort of antidote to all the downers, like a sweet, small, touching thing that happened every year for as long as I lived in Illinois. There was always a single red rose on Sharon's grave on her death day. I don't know who was responsible for that; I never saw the person. I wish I could thank him or her for that remembrance. It was nice to know someone besides me missed her and visited her.

Over the years I have struggled with whether or not to move Sharon out here to Montana with me. I decided for a very long time that she lived and died in Illinois, so that was where she belonged. It has been difficult to get back to visit her grave since we live so far away. We did go back east to my fiftieth high school reunion in 2009 and stopped at the cemetery on the way. It had probably been five or six years since I had been able to get there. It was as hard as ever, and I decided then that I want Sharon here with me. It is no longer about her; now it is for me. I don't know if that will ever really happen, but that was my strong feeling at the time. The reality of disinterring her coffin, shipping it to Montana, and reburying her seems daunting. I don't even know if it would be legal. I suspect the cost and hassle would be enormous. Again the internal conflict: to hold on or let go. So far, I have let her be.

If you
cannot
stand
the
screaming,
get out
of
the
way.

You cannot
resurrect
my
dead child.

I cannot
smile
for
you.

I can
only
smile
after
the
screaming.

It is hard to know what the long-term impact of a tragedy is on an adult. I remember wondering over and over if it was possible to damage an adult, as it is a child. I felt like I had lost my way and couldn't get back to the path, but was wandering around trapped in some thorny patch. I am often surprised by random bouts of guilt or memories that still intrude into my daily life. They seem so incongruent with the rebuilding I have worked so hard on. I realize each of those episodes has occurred when I was drifting from my way, and so they have been a reminder not to get complacent or ever stop growing. Those wrenching times have usually snapped me out of a thorny patch. The danger for me has been not to get bitter and cynical, or totally withdraw.

Fortunately, I am surrounded by family and friends who hold me accountable when I head in a downward direction. Morrie especially is apt to demand that I show up and be present. Morrie has never scolded or admonished me for my struggles, but he does confront me strongly when I begin to abandon myself, and therefore him. As the years march on, it is sometimes hard to make the connection that what is really going on has something to do with grief. The urge to heal and not be in pain is a very powerful force in human life, so the inclination is to hide the discomfort. I remember realizing how much I was looking forward to any excuse to drink because I knew that would numb the pain for a while. That realization really scared me, because I didn't want an alcohol problem on top of everything else. It took a few more years to stop smoking. As long as I kept grieving, I didn't need crutches.

My grief has taken many forms of expression since the first year, during which it manifested as crying. Another form of expression for my grief is the poems I wrote and my endless journaling. Writing is a native tool for me and has helped a lot over the years. It still does. Probably the most amazing aspect of keeping current with my sorrow is the flip side: new depths of appreciation for life, joy in small delights, and a richness in relationships I did not know was possible.

Oh, mystery of life
that I
should
feel such
anguish,
such despair,
&
ever
smile again

But I did begin to smile again, with a little more acceptance of my loss, and growth under my belt. Some resolution came in the form of a series of dreams. The first series was about Sharon still being alive, and I would awaken to the terrible truth of her death and be distraught for hours. The second set was about her being hurt or ill, and I just needed to fix her up or give her the right medicine. Those were hard also. The final set was about her showing up and me saying, "What are you doing here? I know you are dead. Now I just have to go through it all over again." Somehow, exploring Sharon's death in my sleep provided integration for deeper healing. Even my unconscious knew the truth. I don't know if that was a choice or not, but my "stuckness" eased and I was "better."

CHAPTER 4

Twenty Years: No One Cares;

Holding Up Is Hard

Who cares about a twenty-year-old tragedy? Only those of us who have lived it. I have never achieved the "chirpiness" that I see so many wounded folks present; the perpetual smile they show, no matter what is happening.

The death of my child
leaves me
in
a different world

I feel
set apart
somehow.

My choice

to

face

her

death

has opened

secrets

I

did not know

were there.

As I built my career as a psychotherapist, the ability to em-pathize with grief certainly increased, as did my understanding of what people felt. I know that I am often considered tough, hard, or cold and aloof. I have often heard over the years when I give clients tough feedback, "That wasn't very nice." That used to trouble me for days, until I realized they were right; I am not very nice. That is not why people seek me out or stay as my clients. They count on my honest, direct, and real responses. At some point I decided that perfection was no longer a goal; being genuine and authentic is. Seeking perfection is a setup to feel like a failure; reality is possible when I can stay current with my feelings. The biggest surprise has been how much all my grieving has opened me up to all that is beautiful and wonderful about this world. There is a depth and richness which was not there before. My appreciation for others and their struggles is greater, and I stop to smell the roses more often. I guess this is the "payoff" for my choice to grieve.

For those
of us
who are
bereaved,
&
insist
on
facing
our grief,

Life has
a
quality
the
protected
can never
know.

That deeper quality in life is a result of the redoing of reality that sudden, shocking loss requires. Any significant loss requires a lot of internal reorganizing, as one's philosophy is turned upside down; sudden, shocking loss only intensifies this process. Priorities shift and tolerances change. It is backward for me to outlive my child. I am inept and incompetent because I couldn't save my child. In the face of death, we are inept and incompetent; that truth was chilling. So went the internal dialogue. For me, the hardest thing was to be really angry with Sharon. It took me a long time to get to that feeling. How could I be angry with someone who was dead? Especially since I still struggled with the degree of my own complicity in her death. It finally just came, unbidden, with no fanfare or warning. I was visiting her grave for the thousandth time and this rage started at my toes, moved through my gut, and came out my mouth in the form of screaming. I was jumping up and down on her grave. I was truly out of control. It probably lasted all of a few minutes, but it felt like forever. After my outburst I felt really bad and guilty, not knowing exactly what to do next to get back in control or feel better. As I stood there, dazed and in a haze, I slowly calmed down and came out of my rage and despair. The extreme expression of feelings had worked its magic once more.

I am
so
angry,

I feel
so
cheated,

That she
didn't
give
me
one more
chance.

The second stage of grief is anger, the need to place blame, which is related most closely to feelings of helplessness, and is the attempt to regain some sense of control. Anger can often be disguised or misplaced, emerging as an upset sense of reality, characterized by obsessive reviewing. The obsessive review is woven throughout recovery and is like talking the event to death. The grieving person may insist on talking about old times a thousand times, and have little tolerance for others' problems and no interest in others' lives. There is frequently a verbalized statement that "no one has suffered as much as I have." I actually lived this stage myself. Knowing the process and having the intellectual understanding doesn't make the feelings any easier. I don't know how many times I went through the grief cycle. Many. Each time I came out more whole, with some new awareness and healing.

Why is it so important to express anger after a death? There are so many arguments not to: it's not fair; the dead aren't here to defend themselves. It's selfish and not very nice. They didn't die on purpose. Not expressing anger, at its worst, leads to bitterness and cynicism, and at its least creates a distance that is unbridgeable. This is because you can't be safe and intimate at the same time. That would be like trying to be safe while rock climbing; both intimacy and rock climbing require exposure and vulnerability. I don't think anger is any more important than any other feeling or stage of grief, but it seems to be the most difficult to experience. Perhaps it is so difficult because it breaks one of the last ties to the beloved person. All the messages and pressure to avoid conflict makes it scary to express anger.

Life
goes on
&
so
do I.

As though
Sharon
never
existed.

Except,
I
know
she
does.

CHAPTER 5

Twenty-Five Years: Silence and Loneliness;

What More Is There to Say and Do?

I keep
her
things around,
stored
in
boxes
in
the basement-

As though
she
were
simply
away
for a while-

Because
getting rid
of
them
feels like
getting
rid
of her.

After this long a time, there was no one that was even a tad sympathetic, let alone empathetic. Sometimes the loneliness and longing for Sharon was overwhelming. I spent many an hour just sitting with some small memento of her, remembering. This came very close to enshrining her in my own private way. Some families are overt about that and don't change the child's room for years, if ever. Most have something around to remind and remember. The mementos I kept, and keep, were an integral part of my healing and have changed over the years. At first I kept everything I could near me. Pictures, her hairbrush that smelled like her, the funeral bulletin, her obituary, and all her music tapes. As the years have passed, the paraphernalia has condensed to a few pictures from babyhood and the last picture I took of her. Many things are still at hand, but not used as much. Her scent faded from the hairbrush, and other things come and go as I celebrate and grieve each year.

Then there are those that never grieve or speak about their dead child again. This is very hard on families, especially other siblings. A death in the family irrevocably changes everything—the family structure and relationships, to name a few. What that adds up to is, without grieving or processing the loss, the sibling loses every- thing overnight. Without talking about the loss, the impact on the surviving sibling(s) is even more destructive. They have not only lost a brother or sister, they end up losing themselves. As the years go by, reaching each other becomes like trying to shout across the Grand Canyon. The tragedy of the death is compounded by the burden of silence.

It was during the twenty-sixth year that I developed breast cancer, which was an entirely new problem to grapple with. How to fit that into this whole recovery scenario? There were moments when holding up was hard. I had a difficult time reconciling these two life-changing events. It felt like an earthquake. I remember a persistent image I had of myself, sitting in front of a pile of rubble that used to be my life. It was my job to sort through all that and decide what to keep, what to rebuild, and what to let go of. The reaction from those around me (except my inner circle, especially Morrie) was surprisingly similar to when Sharon died. After the surgery and chemo I looked the same. The message was clear: don't talk about it. "Now that it's over, you're OK, right?" It is hard and embarrassing to talk about the fact that after all the intensity and drama of the sequence of events around cancer, it is just over. Since the outcome for me was good, it seems ridiculous to say that going from being the center of attention to no attention was a bit jarring, but there you have it; again the loneliness. That is why my support group was so important.

I am still amazed by how little focus there is on the family members surrounding the patient, like husbands and brothers, as well as friends and everyone else. I was fortunate to have Morrie Shechtman in my corner during those very dark and frightening days. In addition to asking questions I wasn't capable of, in the beginning, he fiercely found the best care available. The hardest part for others to understand is that he was able to tell me how angry he was that I had cancer. Why that is so important is that it made it possible for us to stay close during those terrible months. If he had not, those secret, unspoken feelings would have made everything more difficult, and I would have wondered what was wrong that we couldn't be intimate. There were many other things he felt also, and keeping the relationship honest made the rest possible.

Women who have lost children and have had breast cancer are considered by many to be neither good moms nor sexy. I heard the latter lament over and over from other women in my support group. At some point in this struggle, it occurred to me that life was going to go on whether I did or not, so I might as well join. I have not regretted that choice either. An important piece that helped me through that very difficult time was a persistent sense of being "held up" by all the prayers, good wishes, and positive vibes sent my way. I am not a religious person, but that sense was powerful and difficult to ignore. It was the spiritual equivalent of many hands holding up a person during a "trust fall." I am eternally thankful for all those good wishes. Again, the choice I made was to let people matter and to allow their help to assist me. It is so easy to sink into a private, quiet, internal place that feels safe. The false bargain here is: "If I don't think about her or talk about her, then she won't be so gone."

While fighting breast cancer, my sense of reality was once again upset and I needed to rework my life view one more time. After facing the death of my child, and then my own, my tolerance for political correctness is zero. The flip side of that is that my tolerance for people's grief has increased. I very much understand people trying to hold on to life as they knew it. I am fiercely for a person grieving any way he or she chooses. I once had a young woman client who lost her husband three weeks after they married. Her choice was to wear black for a full year after his death. She got no end of flak from others. Again and again, the message she heard was "get over it"—or, more accurately, "don't bother me."

In the midst
of
my healing
the grief
still comes
sometimes.

Wrenching
tearing
agonizing,
as though
I
found you
dead
today.

Somewhere along the way I became obsessed with what Sharon's death was like. Hard? Easy? What? I also became very curious about the autopsy. It felt like completing some sort of circle, to know the facts. It was important because I had nightmares about how she died, and the very thought of the autopsy made me ill. The autopsy was a state requirement whenever poison was involved, and if there was a question of homicide or suicide. These were agonizing questions to ask and no one wanted to answer them. Today, I could just Google the questions and have the answers in seconds. Not so then. To imagine my child dying all alone was sometimes unbearable, so I needed to know if she had suffered. A friendly nurse finally told me that she probably just went to sleep and never woke up. She also told me what happened during an autopsy. It was a great relief to know that there had not been the mutilation I had imagined.

Another memorable choice point happened during this five-year interval. It was on what would have been her thirty-seventh birthday. I was deeply feeling the silence and loneliness, and shared that with Deb, a dear friend of mine, one of the few people I have shared the poems with. She said she was coming up to spend some time with me. A little while later, she showed up on my doorstep with a wonderful surprise: a birthday cake for Sharon and fifteen balloons, one for each year of her life. Deb helped me celebrate Sharon's life. It is still hard to write about that day through my tears; I was, and still am, so touched by her joining me for a short time. We sat on the deck and cut the cake; one piece for her, one for me, and one for Sharon. I wondered what to do with Sharon's piece; Deb suggested that I throw it over the deck. So we ate our cake and heaved the rest over the side of the deck. At first that seemed strange, but it was another small step in letting go, even of a piece of cake. Besides, Sharon would have thought that was very funny.

Later, we went outside with the balloons, to the other side of the house, not sure why. I remember wondering what to do with all those balloons. Deb suggested I just let them go. She started the whole process by letting go of one balloon and shouting, "I'm sorry I never knew you!" That was another of those emotionally agonizing moments—to hold on or let go. I finally said OK. As she handed me each balloon, I shouted something and released it. One was "I love you!" Two was "I hate you!" Three was "I miss you!" Four was "I'm mad at you for leaving me!" Five was "Let me go!" Then I released the rest all at once. We stood there together and watched them sail away till they were all gone. With each balloon I let her go a little bit more, again, and the final release of the other ten felt wonderful. The silent choice was to open my heart a bit wider for that healing closeness that happens in intimate moments.

I am so grateful for Deb's friendship. That tension will always be there, between letting go of the pain, but never her. Those precious moments ease the tension for a while.

Sometimes I
am tired
of grieving
&
protest so much
pain

I cannot seem
to
ever get
finally through

Roz said,
"Don't try."

"The pain of her
death
is part
of
keeping her
alive
in
you."

CHAPTER 6

Thirty Years: Back to the Beginning; a

Renewed Sense of Purpose and Meaning

The most
creative
task
I have
ever
accomplished,
is
to find
new
meaning
&
value
out of
the
absurdity
of
her death.

There is a sixth stage of grieving, which I have only seen once in all my research and reading, that is called "in memoriam." It is the need to do something creative, useful, and meaningful—to make some personal meaning out of an event that seems meaningless. There are many examples of this; things such as foundations, support groups, books, etc. This writing is mine.

Throughout my life, over these past thirty-plus years, there have been transformational moments. These experiences usually happened for me at the end of a particularly gut-wrenching decision. These times feel to me like I have an existential crisis of some sort, and I come completely unglued. The transformation is putting all the pieces back together, but in a different order. I have often had the mental image during these instances of a very large illuminated egg floating in space; the egg slowly comes apart in large floating pieces. The eggshell pieces rearrange themselves and then come back together as a whole egg again, just in a different configuration. I know I am different from those moments on. The choice to rejoin the human race after the cancer was one of those times. The despair I felt at not being able to reconcile those two upheavals was somehow resolved.

Today
I noticed
I
was smiling
&
not thinking
about
my dead
child.

Does
that mean
I don't
love her?

An important aspect of the redoing of my reality has been the emergence and subsequent living of my values. A lot of that clarity came out of my struggle to be seen as "nice" and to be liked. It was important for me to understand why I couldn't be like everyone else. The journey has been lonely enough, but I also felt the added burden of rejection. I was having a lot of trouble relating to most people. For a long time I assumed it was because of my grief. It was quite a surprise when I began to realize I didn't like them any better than they liked me. It turned out to be a clash of values. Again and again, the push back to me was that I was too harsh, or too blunt. Perhaps that is true, but it does not explain all the disagreements. What it does explain was my insistence on continuing to grieve, even this long after Sharon's funeral. The choice to grieve reflects my value of growth over comfort.

Thirty years seemed, at the time, like a momentous milestone. I have no idea how many times I have cycled through the grieving process. It is never a one-time deal. It is never neat and tidy, nor in any particular order. The only two stages that have any order are the first (shock and denial) and the last (acceptance). The rest are a continual swirl (anger, bargaining, and depression), and often are an unarticulated reaction that doesn't make sense to others. For example, every time I hear the song "You Are My Sunshine," I burst into tears and leave the room. That was a song I sang to Sharon often as she was growing up.

You are my sunshine, my only sunshine
You make me happy when skies are grey
You'll never know dear how much I love you
Please don't take my sunshine away

My reaction makes no sense to anyone but me.

Sometimes,
I forget
&
turn a corner
&
there is a
young girl
that
looks like
her
&
I am
stunned
all over
again.

The second-hardest stage (right behind anger) for everyone is depression, mostly because it is so private and internal. To those around the person it looks very withdrawn and sad. Surprise! He or she is very withdrawn and sad. This is when all the reworking is done, which is why it is so quiet. Most of the time the work is done unconsciously; I often felt like there was a part of me that was off recomputing myself. I went through all the right motions, said all the correct things, but I was not present in what I was doing.

I often had strange thoughts. For example, I remember wondering why my feelings were so extravagant and went on for so long. I would have tried to do a better job of parenting for half the suffering. That led to wondering why we have feelings at all. What good are feelings, anyway? That's not the sort of thing one talks about, not with anyone I know, at any rate. These thoughts felt like random musings to distract me from myself. All that musing and searching led to my developing a theory of human behavior that has served my clients and me well, but that's for another book.

The depressive phase of grief is very important. It is hard to allow people to have that solitude because it also shuts everyone else out. This is the rebuilding time after a shattering experience, and involves putting together all the bits and pieces that take so long to accept. Fortunately, it is usually not continuous; there are times of lightness and fun in between the bouts of soul-searching and rethinking.

My child died
of drugs,
trying to
expand
her
consciousness.

Dealing with her
death
has
expanded mine

far, far
beyond
&
has
made reality
possible.

My personal expansion of consciousness has always been about learning and trying to increase my ability to understand and connect with my clients and others. People struggle to find the words to say what they feel, so I help them articulate the fuzziness and speak the unspoken. That is my basic purpose and meaning in life, to help my clients articulate their experiences and therefore make new choices from that awareness.

CHAPTER 7

Thirty-Five Years: Continuations;

Don't Know What Else to Do; the

Relationship with My Dead Daughter

Over the years, the requirements of my grieving have waxed and waned, but there is always some demand to acknowledge several important dates. The honoring no longer has to be long or dramatic; it just has to be addressed. The relationship I have developed with my daughter over the long haul feels peaceful and bittersweet. I keep the grief in my pocket and take it out from time to time, but it no longer rules my life. It has been a gradual process of choices that have built up over time, like a coral reef. Each individual animal—or choice, in my case—is small and insignificant, but the sum total is breathtaking, though invisible on the surface. By now there is little drama left, and less and less to say. All the building and changes are under the surface. A reef and the human spirit are both easy to shatter, but both are also resilient and tend to rebuild in changed forms. Many other losses have occurred along the way, each with its own pain and recovery. Nothing comes close to the upside-down, inside-out world that the death of my child wrought. What is breathtaking is the healing.

This seems like as good a place as any to include a word or two about the healing power of music, movies, art, and poetry. There are certainly other modes to healing, but these have been especially important to me. The grandness of Beethoven's Fifth Symphony (at full volume) has always provided a place of solace and comfort. Thinking of his tragedy and how he composed while going deaf inspired me to make it through one more day. There is a song Roberta Flack sings called "Jesse" that captures the intense longing for her return that will never happen.

A couple of movies have helped me through the rough times; *Mask* is one. The love and courage portrayed by the character Cher plays in that movie touches my own love for my child. *What Dreams May Come*, starring Robin Williams, is all about grief, recovery, and redemption.

There are many more books and poetry that have been woven through these thirty-plus years in the (sometimes daily) choice to go on and thrive. The point is that I learned to use any and all resources at my disposal to "get on with getting on."

In the beginning
I felt
overwhelmed
&
longed for
the
time I
would

be
healed.

Now that
I am.
I
feel strange,
as though
I
got rid
of
her
somehow.

I remember a long period of time when I was looking for a target; someone to blame, and something to hit. I aimed my unhappiness at several places over the years—her school, the drug dealer, her father—anyone but myself. That was the flip of the guilt regarding my own responsibility. I was never able to sustain that focus because it really didn't help, nor did I feel any better. It finally occurred to me that there would never be any restitution. Nothing could equal that loss nor make me whole again. Ultimately, it felt like an avoidance of the truth not to acknowledge that my loss was final. Blaming anyone was not going to bring her back. Another of those small choices slipped in almost unnoticed, until I realized I was less agitated, more at peace within.

As I sit here debating what else to say, I wonder if writing this is like continually picking the scab off an old wound that I won't let heal, or if it is like resetting a bone that never healed properly. I actually don't know what healing properly should look or feel like for a loss of this nature.

What I have found most helpful over the years are those that chose to be straight with me. It is the silence and abandonment that adds to the pain. I always thought it was a hilarious statement for people to say, "I was afraid that I might upset you." How much more upset can a person be? The protocols for funerals and mourning are pretty thin to nonexistent. Perhaps a word or two about the importance of funerals and graves would be appropriate here. Before Sharon's death, I remember being very critical of funerals, cemeteries, and mourners. I thought it was a lot of fuss about nothing. I guess it is, for those who have not faced a death in the family. It is not really possible to convey bereavement to the non-bereaved.

The funeral is about the final good-byes and making the loss real. It is also a place to celebrate life. Without that there is no closure, which explains why the MIA-POW movement is still active. I have found her graveside a very important place to remember, grieve, and recover.

During the viewing I spent many hours with her body—touching and caressing her, and accepting the reality. There were many that did not want me near her and her coffin; fortunately, Morrie ran interference for me to make that possible. I still don't understand the strange reaction of people to bodies. This was my child's body and I was not afraid of or put off by her remains. I met with several of her friends during that time and they were wonderful. I have lost track of them over the years, so a salute to those of you who hung in during that time. I was always very touched by the number and variety of mementos that were left in her casket. Little treasures they had shared during the times together in Sharon's life.

After all these years I am still grateful to the Hickory Hills, Illinois, police and coroner for their handling of the situation and me. When I was finally able to call them, I was hysterical and distraught; they remained calm and reassuring. They didn't rush me or scold me, just let me tell them what had happened. The coroner took charge and saw to it that I got to see her one more time before they removed her body. He was the one who explained to me that the terrible blotches on her face and arms were from *livor mortis*, when the blood pools in the low points of the body. More information than I ever intended to know about death. I regret that I didn't put that information together in a meaningful way until years later, so I never thanked those people to my satisfaction.

As I write this chapter, it occurs to me that what is left to say is now more outward than inward. To share my story and comfort those that are on my path seems like the "more to do."

CHAPTER 8

Other Losses

There is another population of parents I believe are overlooked and underserved, whose loss is just as heart wrenching. I first encountered these brave people when I worked with Easter Seals. They are the parents of handicapped children. At that time the focus was concentrated on the child, especially those from birth to age three. Everything was still new and baffling to many parents; the need to know, to understand, was paramount in their thinking. Though there is a lot of support for the various aspects of being handicapped, I am not aware of support for the grieving process for these families. It seems to me that the magnitude of their losses equals a death, but is protracted since no one died, only the precious dreams for "my child." There is as much variation in parents' responses to a bedridden child as to anything else life deals out. My heart goes out to those who grieve without knowing it, and suffer without understanding why.

I tried to start a support group for those families and no one ever showed up. No matter what I offered or used to entice people,

I never succeeded in getting even one person to attend. Finally, one very sweet parent told me that while she appreciated my attempts, when people are dealing with the life and death of their child every day, feelings were a luxury they could not afford. So, I learned to spend time with the individual parents. She was right, of course, but the isolation and loneliness these parents lived with was staggering. Some had support from family, friends, and their community, but at the end of the day, they were on their own. I think much has happened for families since then in terms of aid, accessibility, and support, but like for me, in the long haul, it is often tough.

The eighteen and older group of handicapped children were a different story altogether. The years between three and eighteen were the schools' responsibility, so I didn't see as much of those families. After the children turned eighteen, I saw them a lot. Many of those families were worn-out and worn down, but were still expected to act like any other parent. Grief was etched in their faces and language. The tolerance for handicaps in this culture is about equal to the tolerance for grieving, maybe even less.

I have had many parents of handicapped children in my practice over the years, and while the circumstances and specifics are all unique, the struggles are universal. Probably the strongest feelings I have heard are about guilt and shame, with maybe a bit of horror thrown into the mix. The choices these families have to make and live with are often those that suck the least. I remember working with the mother of a child with cerebral palsy; she could barely look me in the eye, feeling so overwhelmed and responsible for the difficult birth that may or may not have caused the damage. The whole family, including the extended family, was struggling with the reality of his appearance, behavior, and limitations. The hardest part was the big secret: the negative feelings they could not express nor deny. She even felt guilty for seeking my help, as she believed it took the focus away from him. Besides, she felt she didn't deserve happiness. Her important work was to sort out the tangled logic that kept her trapped. We talked often about the difference between hating the disability, but not the child; about setting appropriate limits and boundaries, about how to handle all the crises that come with a limited family member, and about her isolation and loneliness. As she was able to get some clarity and relief, she had a funeral for the child of her fantasy, so she could love the child she had. A funeral for a handicapped child has been too difficult for many of my clients, but achieving some form, that they chose, of acceptance that the child would never "get better" allowed them to plan for their future. Until there is some letting go of the past, they are just stuck. All parents of handicapped children are heroes in my estimation.

I also know, from firsthand experience, about living with handicapped family members. I don't have a handicapped child, but I had a handicapped parent. My dad had polio when he was two, so he had a shriveled leg. He walked with a noticeable limp and always used a cane. People were civil, but whispered behind his back. Folks were not so careful about what they said around kids.

Over time, Dad talked about his handicap. He related that when he was a child, the kids made fun of him (called him "crip") and would run away from him. As his child I found that excruciating. I can't imagine what his parents felt. It was very painful watching him struggle to walk, to keep up. My dad was a Methodist minister, so we prayed a lot for a miracle for him. My "wish upon a star" was that he could have two good legs. I have an abiding love and tenderness for him; I mourn the wounds and celebrate the gifts he gave me. One of my dad's proudest accomplishments was that he learned to water-ski, even with his game leg! We have some wonderful pictures of three generations of Hotchkisses waterskiing.

Dad was ahead of his time in that he sought counseling, which took some of the edge off his pain. As an adolescent I found him embarrassing. Fortunately, I outgrew that. The worst part of a handicapped family member is the helplessness to "make it better." Sometimes, as a child, it was hard to understand Dad's rage and essential aloneness. I do now. Finding people that can tolerate me, and those like me, is always my challenge. It was Dad's, too.

It is worth reiterating that grief is just plain brutal, and has honed my life in ways that I often dislike and rail against. However, the alternative of not going on is worse. For me, there were times over these thirty-odd years when I just sat down on the sidelines. I was out of oomph. Slowly, that began to feel like living in a glass jar. I could see and hear everyone and everything, but I could touch no one, and no one could touch me. This was an attempt to feel safe, another bargain. If I just sit quietly, I'll be fine. Living as if one is in a mayonnaise jar may be safe, but it is very lonely and brittle. Breaking out of that jar required me to get up off the bench and re-engage, which of course meant more pain, more grieving. Each time I have cracked the jar I have found new comfort and joy also. They go together.

There is something about the healing power of grief that is almost mystical. I have witnessed over and over again that every breakthrough my clients or I have ever made is always after some important grief work. The truism here is that if you can't grieve, you can't change.

I can't
seem
to stop
writing
these poems.

That's
because
I can't
seem
to stop
living.

Conclusion

In my attempt to express feelings that words can only approximate, each chapter has been a unique struggle to write. The chronology is probably not exact. It's anybody's guess as to what this journey will be about in the coming years and decades. I only know that the learning, growing, and healing will continue. What I do believe is that the journey is easier from all my grieving. Sharon's death contained a strange gift for me, in that I learned how to live from my gut. I think and feel that that is what has made my life rich and full. Many lessons and surprises have come along the way, but what stands out most for me is the stark difference between those who grieve and those that don't.

Of the five basic feelings that come with our humanness (mad, sad, glad, hurt, and afraid), sadness is of the longest duration. None of us can really escape the power of these intense feelings, though we try our darnedest. I am continually amazed by all the pharmaceuticals invented to avoid feelings, especially those connected to grieving. The drug companies have had to keep adding new drugs on top of old ones in the attempt to help people feel better without their ever having to really grieve.

Grief is one of those words that puts fear in the hearts of grown men. Women can cry, but they struggle with grieving, which has to do with the injunctions females hear about selfishness and upsetting others. It is forbidden for males to cry. Years ago I had about seven men in my practice that all sounded alike in their struggles and fears—so much so that it was eerie. I thought they would benefit from a group. They all agreed and we started to work that way. About six weeks into the group, each man took me aside and, in his own way, said, "I will do anything you ask, just don't make me cry."

The restrictions against grieving are numerous and powerful, and start very early in the socialization of children. I think that those taboos are there because the art of grieving changes a person, from one state of existence to another, like boiling water into steam. But steam can be condensed back into water; the change in people is irreversible and permanent. I am awed by the powerful taboos against grieving. I know about this from my work with people and my own struggles to grieve openly.

People have often expressed a deep, abiding fear that if they start grieving they will never stop—or worse, just be stuck in a funk. I have never worked with a person that didn't continue with his or her life as usual while going through this healing process. I have deep respect for those who make that choice. I see how much strength and courage it takes to be that vulnerable and exposed.

What I would like to see happen with this book is the creation of safe places for people to grieve without being interrupted or scolded. The only partially safe place is a cemetery. It would be nice to bring back the notion of the ancient wailing wall. The only thing I have ever experienced that even comes close to what I would hope for is the Vietnam Veterans Memorial Wall in DC. Loved ones are permitted to bring little memorials and at least weep quietly. I would wish for every bereaved person a safe place for deep, healing grief and reflection, in the daunting work of rebuilding a life.

I hope this book has helped you make some sense of your journey, and let a little sunshine in through the clouds.

On the Other Side of Grief

Introduction

During the years since 1978, I have heard a refrain that troubles me and seems unfair. It's the frequent response from those around the bereaved person. So often I hear people say, "Oh, I was just a friend," or, "I am just the cousin." As though their grief isn't as valid somehow. It is. I don't know how one measures the degree of pain felt for the death of a loved person. "Mine can't be as bad as theirs" is what I hear at times. Perhaps—who knows? But whatever degree of pain anyone feels is as important to his or her life as it is to the central figures in the tragedy. In answer to that mistaken assumption I wrote the following article, "On the Other Side of Grief," for all those who are on the other side yet part of the inner circle. Shutting down grief always creates distance and safety; getting close risks being vulnerable to loss once again.

Just as grief is the natural and normal human response to loss, so is our response to a grieving person. It is very difficult to see someone we know who has experienced a great loss and not want to do something to help. Both grief and the response to grief have gotten lost along the way. This essay, then, is about describing and supporting our natural and normal responses to someone else's grief. It is a parallel process and embodies similar stages, but requires only the awareness to trust what we can do to help.

This parallel process is important not only to help the bereft person recover, but also to accommodate and create the inevitable new relationship with him or her. Significant loss irrevocably changes people, and therefore any and all relationships. So, part of the helping process is to accept the changed person and relationship along with the loss.

There is so much to say about loss because the range of emotions and behaviors is so enormous. Much has been written in recent years about the stages of grief that have become part of the common wisdom and seem pretty accurate. However, the mourner does not experience stages—just feelings. Often these are strange, unfamiliar, and very intense feelings that people have spent a lifetime learning to control. So reassurance is one of the first responses anyone can give. It is often helpful for people to at least understand what is happening to them. Then they do not have the added burden of thinking something is wrong with them. What is "wrong" is that they have lost something or someone significant.

It seems important to understand that any encounter with a grieving person is unsatisfying. This is so because neither party can give the other what he or she wants. We do not have the power to give back what has been lost, and the grieving person cannot give us the smile and assurance that our help has made everything all right. The greater the loss, the longer this will be true. However, over time our assistance does help. It is analogous to applying salve to a wound. The salve will not magically heal, but over time the salve, plus the healing power of the body, will at some point heal the wound.

What seems important is to recognize some of the signs of mourning and to know we will have a parallel process.

Having dealt with grief from the inside out as a bereaved parent and a bereaved child, and from the other side of grief as a professional, there are a few more things I have learned.

Sudden, shocking loss is one of the most difficult aspects of our humanness. I am talking about any loss, not only death. There is divorce, loss of jobs, loss of health and youth, moving, etc. And the biggest surprise: wonderful events always embody loss. The birth of a child, marriage, a promotion, a new house, and any success mean leaving something behind.

Most people move through grief in the context of family, friends, and community; many with the help of their faith and church. It is only a problem when a person gets stuck in one of the stages. This brings me to the two most common questions asked. The first is: "Well, how long will this take?" or "How long should it take?" The second is: "Is this normal?"

In the attempt to answer these questions, I have defined grief as either acute or chronic. Acute grief is the normal, natural process that people move through. Chronic grief is when the grieving process is shut down and stuck in a particular phase. It doesn't matter how or when this happens; if the process is shut down, it will never be finished.

The first year is the hardest, because it is the anniversary year. Each holiday or special time is the first without the lost person, lost job, lost community, or whatever the particular loss might be. Around the first year anniversary a marked change is usually evident. Not that grieving is done, but the acute submersion is less. I am deliberately not being very specific, because grief is so individualized. To set time frames would compromise the respect and dignity of people's right to grieve in their own time and in their own way. There simply is no logical sequence to all the feelings—they come when they come, and not on schedule.

However, given all that, there are some behaviors that suggest when a person is in chronic grief. Let me step back and say that what makes grief so mysterious and hard is that it cuts right through all the defenses and touches our core. In cutting through, it touches all other grief and unresolved issues and brings them to the surface with the current grief. That is a lot of the sense of being out of control and feeling crazy. If there are significant unresolved issues, the defensive system will go into overdrive, and the result is that a person gets stuck. Much like a record, just going round and round in the same phase. This is also true for those around the grieving person. If we have unresolved issues, we will have a difficult time being around any grief. It is difficult to discern the difference, because "stuckness" is simply an extension of normal, acute grief. The key is that it feels "off" to people around them.

All stages of grief are in service of survival in an adversarial world. This is an ancient demand from when survival was a daily question, so even though our survival is assured, the primitive nature of grief hasn't changed. This is most of the reason why it is so difficult to understand. In a rational culture, the irrational is viewed with suspicion and disdain.

In an attempt to make sense of this dissonance, I have created the Change Spiral, which is a visual aid for a simple gut experience. This process applies to any change, good or bad, and anyone can see where he or she is on the spiral. For a long time, the swirl of feelings feels more like a whirlpool or a tornado than a simple spiral, so I have flattened it out for practical purposes.

Each point on the spiral represents a time frame that is elastic, but limited, and the movement is often imperceptible to others and to ourselves.

The Change *Spiral*

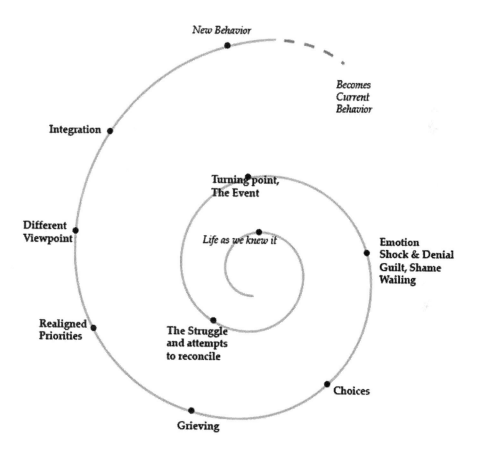

Life as We Knew It – Emotions – Choices

In the center of the spiral is life, as we knew it, which is followed by all the actions we tried and attempts we made to keep everything the same. In the event of an accident, this is often the "if onlys" and "what ifs" recriminations that we fantasize could have changed the outcome. As we move around the spiral we come to the choices. This should actually look like a web, as it is difficult to know which way to go, and it is easy to get trapped in one of the arms.

Grieving

The next point is grieving itself, which is essentially an invisible, intangible, and immeasurable internal experienced that is difficult to share. The rest of the spiral is benchmark points that create the long-term consequences of change. This is why people resist change (grief); it is hard, even brutal, and very unsafe—unsafe in the sense that life is no longer predictable, measured, or secure.

Realigned Priorities

As people move around the spiral they find that what was important a year ago seems to fade in the background or may seem trivial. These old issues grow into new awakenings, avenues, and endeavors. In short, most of our priorities are realigned. For me, this is where I began to find political correctness less and less tolerable, and my relationships more precious. I found myself more open with people I care about, and more confrontational and demanding, as I didn't want anything left unsaid or undone ever again.

Different Viewpoint

As priorities shift and realign, it leads to all sorts of tangled feelings, thoughts, and outcomes. Our point of view is like a kaleidoscope; all the pieces are the same, but what and how we see the world is ever squiggling. This is quite unnerving, as it is hard to predict our own reactions anymore, and that is downright scary. My own political viewpoint began to slide across the spectrum of liberal to conservative, which required a whole renegotiation with the world I lived in. All of this happens over a period of years, so the new outlook was gradual. I don't know what life would be like if Sharon hadn't died, but what I do know is what I have rebuilt has been worth the effort. Through all the grieving, where I finally landed is in the present, a very nice place to live.

Integration

I have always seen my life as a journey through a dark and scary forest, where there are all sorts of obstacles, cliffs, and wild beasties to deal with. Every once in a while I come to a meadow—the sun is shining, the grass is green, and it is good to be alive. That is when the integration of all the hard labor is accomplished and I get to rest for a while. What I know about myself is that at some time I'm going to get tired of the meadow, look up and say, "Gee, I wonder what's over that ridge," and plunge right back into the forest. This meadow corresponds to the acceptance and in memoriam stages of grief.

New Behavior – Current Behavior

Any new behavior emerges out of the previous points along the way. New behaviors, like standing up for myself better, grew out of feeling more confident that I can deal with the forest, which grew from accepting that, sadly, I can never go back to the way I was. This was an important choice point: to decide whether to go on or shut down. This, then, becomes current behavior, which leads right back to the center of the spiral and starts all over again with any significant change in our lives. Less significant change is simply a smaller spiral. With the pace of change in our world today, there are commonly several spirals going on at the same time, certainly adding to our sense of stress.

Stage 1

The first stage of grief is shock and denial. This stage is characterized by feeling and acting chaotic. Often a person will say that he or she feels crazy or disorganized. Often it will be difficult for the person to concentrate and stay focused. This is usually exacerbated by cultural norms that require life to go on and for the person to be "tough." The internal experience just does not fit, so the person feels guilty or ashamed that he or she does not have better control. No words can capture the full depth and intensity of grief, so the person has a great deal of trouble defending himself or herself from these messages.

The people around often have similar reactions, wanting to minimize and make things OK. There is usually a sense of great helplessness. This is often captured in the phrase "I don't know what to say." This is shock and denial on our part. The mind freezes and we draw a blank. It is the "Oh no, this can't be true," and (in a secret place), the "I don't want to deal with this." Denial is important and necessary in the beginning. At times, we know the truth before we totally accept it. Shock and denial protects us from being totally overwhelmed, and then the dealing with it comes in small, manageable pieces. This is why it takes so long.

It is difficult to give a time frame for stages, since each person is unique, and the shift from one stage to another is usually gradual, seldom sequential, and never neat and tidy. Often, a person will experience all the stages in a whirl from time to time, but each stage has a specific set of tasks that has to do with healing, restructuring, and a characteristic mood or "sense of."

The shock and denial phase of the non-mourners is much shorter and usually passes quickly, and we do think of something comforting to do or say.

People who are stuck (chronic grief) in shock and denial are amazing to be around. They seem strong and in control. We seem to admire them and wish we were that tough. Do not believe it. This type of behavior is necessary and appropriate to get through the first few days or weeks after a loss, to simply accomplish all the practical tasks required. But if there is no reaction, it is a danger sign. This stuckness is characterized by a lack of, or inappropriate, affect or feeling. There is a strange incongruence in affect and behavior that does not fit the circumstances. I have come to call this "chirpy."

Chirpiness is probably the result of a lifetime of "being there" for everyone else and feeling too terrified of the vulnerability of "breaking down" and needing to ask for something from others. Persons stuck in this phase are certainly no trouble to be around. They do not bother anyone with their problems. They are also impossible to get any closer to. A safe distance from others is the rule here, so as not to risk grieving. This is most likely related to early abandonment issues, and as a youngster this person was required to perform far beyond his or her developmental abilities. The way to help someone in this terrible dilemma is to gently insist on closeness. In short, to offer the help this person is so terrified of asking for.

Stage 2

The second stage of grief is anger, which is related most closely to feelings of helplessness, and is the attempt to regain some sense of control. Anger is often disguised or misplaced. Sometimes emerging in this stage is an upset sense of reality, characterized by obsessive reviewing. The obsessive review is woven throughout recovery and is like talking the loss and the event, literally, to death. The person may insist on talking about old times a thousand times, and have little tolerance for other's problems and no interest in other's lives. There is frequently a verbalized statement that "no one has suffered as much as I have."

This phase is also characterized by the need to place blame. A great deal of time and energy is invested in trying to figure out why this loss happened and what or who "caused" it. This is another attempt to reduce the pain. It is also a way of trying to hold on to life as they knew it. The time and energy is a distraction from reality for a little while.

It is so difficult to be angry directly—especially at the dead person. It is hard to be angry with someone you cared for, who didn't decide to die. It is so difficult because anger exposes our needs and our fear of weakness with it. This makes us feel terribly vulnerable and exposed.

Our response is often feeling angry, fed up, and even disgusted. We feel angry at the person's passivity, inappropriateness, or self-absorption. We are sick of hearing about it. We feel angry that nothing we do seems to help, and we just want them to get on with life. This is an important turning point in the process, and the most important thing we can do is to say exactly what we feel. This truly helps the person move into the next stage, and keeps the connection of the relationship alive and growing. If we turn away because we do not want to add to the burden or upset him or her more, we begin to create distance. The grieving person is then even more isolated and alone.

People who are stuck (chronic grief) in anger are very easy to spot. They are often bitter, blaming, and sometimes cynical. Those stuck in the anger phase of grief are difficult to be around. Though they often do not ask for much emotionally, they may be overly demanding in other ways. The purpose, or attempt, here is to feel safe and back in control. The task for this phase is to break free of the attachments that no longer exist so healing can occur. Once again, chronicity creates distance. Anger of this nature is probably related to early betrayal of the child. As a youngster, this person was most likely required to protect others from their own needs or pain. So grief elicits enormous guilt and shame at one's impotence. Helplessness is very hard to deal with, particularly for men. A lifetime of being in charge and knowing how to "fix" life can be profoundly compromised when faced with loss. This is very frightening and may cause internal panic, in the form of rage. Few men have the understanding or emotional skills to deal with intense loss. The way to help people stuck in anger is to help articulate the bind they are in and how unfair it all is, that they have to change or retreat. Otherwise, they are profoundly alone and isolated, and believe they are different or strange.

Stage 3

The next stage to be discussed is bargaining, which is a deep regression to an earlier, much younger state. We often see strange rituals, enshrinement, or deification that all seem puzzling or obscure. This is primitive, magical thinking, and also the attempt to regain some sense of control or "normalcy." There is the need to feel safe, and there is no safety. The work during this phase is to realize that nothing will bring back life as you have known it, no matter how many things are enshrined. This is a very important time and is part of the redoing of the upset sense of reality. It is an "if this, then that" attitude. For example, in bereavement we sometimes see a room or object enshrined; the thrust being, if I keep everything exactly as it was, then the person will not be so gone.

In this stage, the grieving person's and the helper's response is to bargain for impact; to try and do something safe and familiar. The most common form this takes is for us to join in the rituals. It is such a relief to feel useful and see the grieving person interacting once more. It seems like the person is finally getting on with life, and he or she is. This joining together continues to strengthen the relationship and is part of our new history together.

A person stuck (chronic grief) in bargaining continues with the rituals, enshrinement, or deification in order to avoid further hurt. I have known parents that haven't touched anything in the child's room since the death, as though that child would return and continue like always. Others I have worked with simply won't talk about the child, as though he or she never existed. These people also do not bother those around them. It is as though everything is OK once again. The problem is that further growth and intimacy is not possible in all other areas of life. This is a very tricky type of stuckness because it is usually not visible to others. The person may appear to be peaceful. The key is the lack of growth, because all energy is being used to stay in place. Sometimes there are clues in unreal conversations about the loss. This phase is probably related to significant earlier loss that is also unresolved and the person is simply overwhelmed. As a youngster, this person was probably required to be stoic or a good soldier. The bargain is usually not spoken, but goes something like "If I do not change anything, it will not be so true." The way to help a person stuck in bargaining is a gentle, but firm, confrontation that life must go on. This type of message may need to be expressed several times. Otherwise, the mourner may sink deeper into isolation and magical thinking.

Stage 4

The next stage is depression. This is usually the longest, lasting up to a year or more in duration. This is often a very private time; the mourner is deeply internalized. It looks like withdrawal—and it is. This is where the major work is done. Sadness, remorse, guilt, weeping, sighing, and a lower level of activity characterize this time. Life feels bleak, futile, and sometimes meaningless. Most people continue to work and do things as usual, but it is like going through the motions. That is because most of the energy is being used to recover, much like recovering from major surgery. There is not much lightness or joy during this time. Depending on the nature and degree of the loss, this is an existential crisis, an identity crisis; one's entire life view is being redone. For example, in dealing with my own bereavement—the death of my fifteen-year-old daughter—the belief that I could protect my children was shattered. I realized about eight months after her death that this loss was no guarantee or insurance that I would not lose again. I realized that I had no exemptions from life, no special privileges. And perhaps the hardest: no restitution. No one would or could make up for or replace what I had lost. I was faced with terrible fear and the choice of whether I wanted to risk loving again. All those thoughts, feelings, and decisions occurred during my very long depression.

This is an equally difficult time for those around the grieving person. Grief goes on longer than anyone wants it to, or thinks it should. Everyone gets sick of it, including the bereft person—and still it goes on. Hang in there, is the message here. It will end, time does heal. As helpers, once again we feel our own helplessness and impotence, and we want to withdraw. That is a normal and natural response, and is to be trusted. Some distance is necessary at this point because so much of the work is private and internal. Just sitting or walking together, or a brief handclasp, is all that is required, and the most effective way to get through this time.

This is the rebuilding time after a shattering experience, and all the bits and pieces that take so long to accept need to be put back together, often in a different configuration. Once again, this is the continued evolution of a new history together.

The last phase a person can be stuck in (chronic grief) is depression. This is really hard to call, because depression is also the longest part of recovery. We often get weary of the length of depression. So much happens during this time; the most significant choice being made is whether or not to pick up and go on with life. A person stuck in depression uses the loss as the reason to stay in place. The loss is used as a sort of brake and a break to keep from moving too fast. Sometimes the person just stops and never seems to get moving again.

I will never forget how a friend of mine helped me move on. About two years after my daughter's death, he commented that I used her death like a black ace, to hide behind. I, of course, was very hurt and indignant at first, but as time passed I realized he was right. Again, it was the attempt on my part to be safe; this time by asserting my pain and wearing it as my shield against caring or involvement with him. It made closeness and comfort impossible. I was a bit wobbly about taking the risk of loving and losing again. To come out of my depression and be there for someone else was reengaging in life and investing in the future. Sometimes the hardest things to say are the kindest. I am glad he and others cared enough for me to want me back.

This is also another example of the new person and new relationship emerging from the old. Because people pursued me, and because I chose to live, I have been able to recover. My goal has become to turn around and give back to others who have just begun their journey.

Being stuck in depression is probably related to an early loss of self. More than any other stage, this may require some additional professional help. It is broader and more pervasive than most other feelings, and harder to define and get to the root. It is amazing to me how many people sense that they are stuck and simply need support to follow through. Perhaps some reassurance that they are not bad or crazy—just stuck for the moment.

In many instances, professional counseling is the only help available. This is due to not having families and communities easily within reach anymore. It is also due to the strange lack of permission in our culture to grieve. The further away from the event, the less it is OK to still feel sad or be mourning. After three to six months the person is expected to be back to normal, and after the first year fewer and fewer people even remember the loss. It takes a good three years to feel comfortable after moving geographically from one home to another, let alone after a death, a divorce, or a major illness. The less tangible and concrete the issue, the more pressure there is to forget it, or the implication that it is only in our head, and not real pain.

Counseling offers a sympathetic ear, supportive assurance, cognitive understanding, and simply a safe place to continue the process. For people to admit they need help, and then to actually go for help, takes enormous courage and strength—because the message is that we should be tough, handle our own problems, and after all, these are "only feelings."

Stage 5

The next stage is acceptance. This is like a sunrise. The grieving person begins to get on with life. Energy and interests, pleasure and joy gradually return. If the grief work has been done for the bereaved person and the helper, there is a new sense of strength and purpose, and the relationship is deeper and wider than before. Both feel OK about the relationship and so are able to connect in new, nourishing, and more productive ways. Both the bereaved person and the friend have to make a myriad of choices to achieve a stage of acceptance. One of the hard lessons learned throughout the healing is that adults often have to learn how to pick the choice that sucks the least.

Stage 6

The final stage is called "in memoriam." This stage is not mentioned much in the literature, but seems to belong because so much has been created out of significant losses. It is the need to do something creative, useful, and meaningful; to create some personal meaning out of an event that seems meaningless and often absurd. There are many examples of this, such as foundations, support groups, books, etc. This kind of writing is mine.

Some Final Notes

Grief cannot be denied; only delayed. When people try to deny and suppress it, grief shows up in physical symptoms, due to the stress of so much control. The physical symptoms most closely related to grief are any number of chronic upper respiratory illnesses. The hard part is that these are also very real diseases. It is more an association than a one-to-one cause and effect. But over the years I have noticed that people who have experienced loss, and not grieved, tend to catch cold more often and their colds last longer.

Grief comes in waves that are relatively short in duration, and very intense. This intense expression of deep feelings leaves one feeling dazed and stunned—briefly—then there is some relief, until the next wave. Between the waves, life goes on as usual. Eventually, the waves of grief get further apart, less intense, and less devastating, like a receding tide. Grief and guilt go hand in hand. Guilt is woven throughout the process. It is profoundly a part of our humanness, and is the result of being imperfect and often impotent. As we face our limitations, the guilt gradually disappears. There is so much in life that we have no control over and no say about. We are stuck with what life deals us. Our freedom is in how we choose to deal with that hand.

Given all the possibilities of how the process can go awry, most people somehow manage to get through and recover—usually with grace and dignity. It is a continual tribute to the human spirit, and I am always impressed.

Poems

Dec 8-11, 1978

Ay, go to the grave of buried love and meditate:

> There settle the account with thy conscious for every past benefit unrequited -- every past endearment unregarded, for that departed being who can never, never, never return to be soothed by thy contrition.

Washington Irving, <u>Rural Funerals</u>

With no explanation or apology, these poems are part of my attempt to deal with the death of my child.

I am astonished
by how
stunned
broken
wounded
I am
by my child's death

I am astonished
by the
depth
breadth
pervasiveness
of my
pain in her loss

I am astonished
by how
the loss
of love
hurts

I am astonished
by how
living
love
heals

Your death has
split me
wide open,
I am gutted
like a steer
freshly slaughtered.

Your death
has spared me
nothing
in horror,
in terror.
in guilt.

What I didn't expect,
had no way
of knowing,
was that the
depth I
plummeted to
would
also find
new depths of
living
&
loving
&
laughter.

Your Precious life
is gone,
some
by your own
hand.

Why?
I do not understand.

I am humbled
by
my own
limitations
that
I
could not
help you want
to live.

I am defeated
by
my own
pain, &
still
I
do not accept
what you said
about me.

Anguish,
Agony.
Screaming pain.

That is my world
my universe.

How do I survive?
Why do I want to?

Because
You are there

I came in one day
&
found Sharon dead
&
I went mad.

Because you were there
&
let me have
my
madness
&
grief
I am healing.

Thank you.

Sometimes I
am tired
of grieving
&
protest so much
pain

I cannot seem
to
ever get
finally through

Roz said,
"Don't try"

"The pain of her
death
is part
of
keeping her
alive
in
you"

You cannot
know
what it's
like
to
have lost
a
beloved child.

You don't
have to
it is
enough
to
hold me
tight
&
let me
cry.

Sometimes
I am
reduced to
nothing
but
my
grief at
loving&
missing
her.

When I am
able
to
let that
be,
I rise,
like
the
Phoenix.

Sometimes,
it is
very
hard.

Sometimes,
I forget
&
turn a corner
&
there's a
young girl
that
looks like
her
&
I am
stunned
all over
again.

Sometimes
I dream
that
she is
still
alive.

Then I awake
&
know
the
truth.

At those
times
I
am
glad
you
are there.

April 1979

The death of my child
leaves me
in
a different world

I feel
set apart
somehow.

My choice
to
face
her
death

has opened
secrets
I
did not know
were there.

My child died
of drugs,
trying to
expand
her
consciousness.

Dealing with her
death
has
expanded mine
far, far
beyond
&
has
made reality
possible.

Expanded consciousness
is simply
dealing
with
the
pain
&
living
my
life.

I am able
to be
reduced
to raw, open
pain
&
come back
whole.

Oh, mystery of life
that I
should
feel such
anguish,
such despair,
&
ever
smile again.

When there
is
no one
there
for
me.

When I
must
face
her death
all alone.

When I
find
her dead
again & again.

That is when
I
know
who
I am.

When I
am
all alone
&
the universe
is
only
mypain & grief.

That is
when
I
know most
deeply
what
it
means
to be
human.

Life feels
futile
&
sometimes absurd.

Why then
do I
go on?

Because, I
love
this world
&
have
to know
what
tomorrow holds.

If you
cannot
stand
the
screaming,
get out
of
the
way.

You cannot
resurrect
my
dead child.

I cannot
smile
for
you.

I can
only
smile
after
the
screaming.

Her death is
no
guarantee,
no insurance,
that I
will
not
lose again.

There is no
way
to
protect myself
from
further loss.

That is deeply
frightening.

What do
I
do with
that?

Well,
I guess
I
notice
how precious
today is
&
how deeply
I love you.

If anyone had
told me
a year ago
that
I
would be
this
healed,
I
probably would
have
slapped them.

Yet I am.

How
astonishing
is
the
human spirit.

In the midst
of
my healing,
the grief
still comes
sometimes.

Wrenching
tearing
agonizing,
as though
I
found you
dead
today.

Last year
I
broke my leg-
got a
divorce-
&
buried my
only
daughter

This year
my
leg is healed-
I am
in love-
&
have recovered
from
her death.

Next year I
plan to
run alot-
perhaps
get remarried-
&
work with bereaved
parents.

Isn't that amazing?

It is
strange
&
blasphemous,
to say
I
have benefitted
from
the grief
of
my child's
death.

It is
also
the
truth.

For those
of us
who are
bereaved,
&
insist
on
facing
our grief,

Life has
a
quality
the
protected
can never
know.

Guilt,
mountains, oceans,
infinite
guilt
that I
failed
my child
so
profoundly
that
she chose
to die.

Ultimately,
I
don't know why.

What I do
know
is
simply that
I did not
hurt
her
as much
as
her death
hurt
me.

Today
I noticed
I
was smiling
&
not thinking
about
my dead
child.

Does
that mean
I don't
love her?

July 1979

I am
so
angry,

I feel
so
cheated,

That she
didn't
give
me
one more
chance.

Life
goes on
&
so
do I.

As though
Sharon
never
existed.

Except,
I
know
she
does.

My blasphemy
is
that
I
can
no longer
remain
distraught.

Is that
a
betrayal
of
her?

In the beginning
I felt
overwhelmed
&
longed for
the
time I
would
be
healed.

Now that
I am.
I
feel strange,
as though
I
got rid
of
her
somehow.

I am
right
between
the depth
of
my grief
&
recovery

A
very
awkward place
to
be.

The most
creative
task
I have
ever
accomplished,
is
to find
new
meaning
&
value
out of
the
absurdity
of
her death.

I guess
I thought
the
depth of
my
grief
was
some measure
of
my love
for
her.

A tiny voice.
deep inside
whispers-
"Living
your life
is
the
only possible
answer
to
death."

I hear
your
laughter
see your
smile,
in
my memory
in
my mind.

I
don't
want
a
memory.

I
want you
alive.

I keep
her
things around,
stored
in
boxes
in
the basement-

As though
she
were
simply
away
for awhile-

Because
getting rid
of
them
feels like
getting
rid
of her.

Dante's Inferno,
doesn't
even
come close
to
the pain
of
my child's
death.

No Hell
imagined
by man,
or
devised
by God,
could
"punish"
me more.

I can't
seem
to stop
writing
these poems.

That's
because
I can't
seem
to stop
living.

About the Author

Arleah Shechtman, M.S.W., A.C.S.W., is a recognized expert on the impact of the death of a child, on marriages, families, and individual survivors. For over thirty years, she has helped parents, siblings, grandparents, and extended family, grieve the loss of their children, and guide them on their journey of recovery. In addition, she has consulted with healthcare professionals whose practices involve working with clients who have lost children through illness, accidents, suicide and acts of crime. Arleah began her own journey of recovery thirty-four years ago, after the death of her fifteen-year-old daughter. She has transformed her own tragedy into a personal and professional mission to create places and resources where those struggling with the death of a child, can find solace, support, and understanding of their irreparable loss.

58727722R00080

Made in the USA
Lexington, KY
17 December 2016